SALES FORECASTING FOR BUSY PEOPLE

16 Easy and Effective Forecasting Techniques

Paul Arinaga

For Dad, a self-made man

TABLE OF CONTENTS

TABLE OF CONTENTS

INTRODUCTION

When I was just starting my career as a newly minted employee of Microsoft back in its heydays, I was asked by my boss to give a presentation. I was to brief a group of software executives from foreign companies on the Japanese software market. As I was a rookie and actually knew very little about the Japanese software market at that point, I was fairly nervous but I went ahead with preparing my presentation nonetheless.

On the day of the presentation, around thirty software executives gathered in a conference room at Microsoft's Tokyo HQ. I started my presentation and it went reasonably well, but halfway through it someone in the group raised his hand and asked for clarification. It was the kind of software guy who is obviously smart and also a little cynical. What this person asked was whether I was presenting installed base or unit sales.

For a moment I was stunned; I was at a loss for words. I didn't know how to answer the question. Why? Because at the time I didn't even know what the difference was between installed base and unit sales! Not wanting to appear like an ignoramus, I hurriedly gave an answer and moved on. Later, I realized that I'd actually given the wrong answer. So, I, the presumed "market expert" had actually misled people.

I consider myself to be well educated and intelligent, but at that point in time I hadn't had any formal education in forecasting techniques. I had an advanced degree in international economics, but I didn't know the difference between installed base and unit sales, and I'd never made a sales forecast before.

The point of this story is that there are a lot of things that are not taught in any school that you nonetheless need to know in the business world. Without this knowledge and these practical skills – especially when you start off in your career or if you change career – you may not actually have the right skills for the job. This is supported by data: according to a recent Gallup poll, only 14% of recent college graduates in the workforce said they felt prepared by their studies. Similarly, only 11% of business executives agreed with the statement that they were getting enough college graduates with the right skills.

In a recent Gallup poll, only 14% of recent college graduates in the workforce said they felt prepared by their studies, and only 11% of business executives agreed with the statement that they were getting enough college graduates with the right skills."

With this book I'd like to help you acquire a very practical skill: how to make a sales forecast.

By reading this book, you'll learn:

- How to make a forecast step-by-step
- 16 fast and effective sales forecasting techniques
- When to use which technique
- How to validate your sales forecast so that it's accurate and credible
- How to present your sales forecast

- "What if's?" or obstacles you may encounter and how to overcome them

The approach: "KISS = Keep it simple, silly!"

I find that people often over-complicate things. Yet particularly in the realm of sales forecasting, it makes no sense to develop overly sophisticated or complex forecasting models. Why? Because a model will only be as good as the assumptions that underpin it and the data fed into it. These are actually far more important than the "technique" used as such.

Thus, the approach used here follows the "KISS" motto: "Keep it simple, silly!" I'm not calling anyone silly. Sophisticated models have their place. Building highly complex models that use sophisticated statistical techniques is usually not a good way to predict sales, however. The level of sales will always be open to interpretation, particularly for new products or in changing markets. There is no point in building a fancy model if your assumptions are flawed or your data is unreliable. Deficiencies in these two areas will probably far outweigh any potential gain in accuracy due to the use of sophisticated modeling or statistical techniques. In short, sales forecasting is probably more "art" than "science".

Keeping it simple means that in order to construct a solid sales forecasting model you don't need to use sophisticated statistical techniques or know high-level math. Basic arithmetic and in some cases a little algebra will usually be all that you need. This means that anyone can create a plausible sales forecast; you don't need an MBA or a degree in advanced economics.

Enough said. Let's get started!

PART I:

Definitions and Cautions

Y ou may want to dive immediately into learning the 16 techniques, but I believe it's important to first ensure that you understand all the key terminology, as well as the most important trends and drivers in your market. A good sales forecast begins with a good understanding of your market.

Volume vs. Value

A fundamental distinction is between volume and value. When we talk about volume we're usually talking about things or "widgets". However, volume could also be something less tangible such as meals, projects or hours. Volume, therefore, can be a thing or an entity. It is typically expressed as "units".

When we talk about value, we're simply talking about money. This could be yen, dollars, pound sterling, euros, bitcoins, or any other currency.

• • •

 Sales by volume rarely lie

When conducting an analysis of sales or when forecasting sales, it's often safer to focus first on sales by volume because sales by value may mask important trends. For example, your sales by value may have gone up, but you may actually have sold fewer units overall simply because you sold relatively more higher-end (i.e. higher-priced) products or because you were able to raise your prices (better price realization). This could have any number of ramifications for your market position. It could mean:

- There is a shift in customer preferences towards higher-end products

- Sales of your lower-end products are being eroded by products from low-cost competitors, but the loss in volume is being made up for by increased sales of your higher-end products

- You're gaining more pricing power or customers are becoming less price sensitive

- There was a change in accounting rules regarding the timing of sales recognition (e.g. a sale is recognized earlier such that sales revenue which would normally be credited in the next period gets credited in the current period)

• • •

Go Granular

It may also be important to examine sales on a more granular level, i.e. in more detail such as by month rather than just by year. For example, imagine that your sales show a sudden increase from one year to the next. There could be several possible explanations for this "bump" in sales such as:

- You made one large sale to a single customer

- There was a seasonal jump in sales

- Your launch of a new product or upgrade to an existing product boosted overall sales

• • •

Installed Base vs. Annual Sales

Another important distinction is between installed base and annual sales, or between penetration and market share. The basic difference is that installed base is what economists call a "stock" while market share is a "flow". Installed base or penetration is like a reservoir of water, whereas annual sales or market share is like a flowing river. Penetration measures the total of your installed base as a percentage of the total market installed based. Market share measures your annual sales as a percentage of total market sales in that year.

Installed base is like a reservoir of water, whereas annual sales is like a flowing river."

Example

Let's suppose that in year one, we sold one unit, and our competition also sold one unit. Thus the total market in year one (i.e. total sales) is comprised of two units. The installed based of the market is two units and our penetration rate is one unit out of the two units or 50%.

Year One	Sales			Installed Base
	Our sales	Competition sales	Total Sales	
	1 unit	1 unit	2 units	2 units

Now let's suppose that in year two in the total market there were sales of three additional units. So now the entire market is comprised of five units; the installed base is now equal to five units. Let's suppose that of those three additional units, we sold two and our competition sold one. That means that now we have three out of the five total units, whereas our competition has two. So our penetration rate of the installed based is 60%, three out of the five units. Because we sold two out of the three units that were sold in that year, our market share is 66.7% or two-thirds.

	Sales	Market share	Installed based	Penetration
Year 1				
Total market	2 units		2 units	
Our company	1 unit	50%	1 unit	50%
Competition	1 unit	50%	1 unit	50%
Year 2				
Total market	3 units		5 units	
Our company	2 units	67%	3 units	60%
Competition	1 unit	33%	2 units	40%

Cautions

Garbage In, Garbage Out

In the IT world, there's a concept called "GIGO" which stands for "Garbage-In, Garbage-Out". The idea is that if the data you feed into a computer is "garbage" the results you'll get out will also be "garbage".

I would argue that the same applies in the forecasting world. If your data is not reliable; if your assumptions are incorrect; or if the logic of your forecasting model is flawed, then the results you get will also be "garbage". In short, your forecasting model is only as good as the data, assumptions and logic that you use to create it. Improve your "inputs" to improve the quality of the insights you get from your sales forecasting model.

Assumptions

It is essential that you make your assumptions explicit. Write all of them down. Contrary to what some may think – and some may do – a forecasting model is not a black box; it should be very transparent.

Examples of assumptions:

- Our product is unique. Competitors will not be able to replicate it. We have a competitive advantage (hopefully, it's true and your competitive advantage can't be eroded over time).

- The overall market will continue to grow by 10% per year.

- If we lower our price by 10%, demand will increase by 30%. In other words, demand is very elastic and sensitive to price.

Understanding market dynamics

People are often focused on achieving the most accurate result possible with their sales forecast, and obviously that's important. Remember, however, that another benefit of engaging in the exercise of building a forecast is that it forces you to better understand how your market actually functions. Therefore, don't focus solely on the end result, your sales numbers. As you construct your

Another benefit of building a forecast is that it forces you to better understand how your market actually functions."

forecast, do also try to understand how the market works. Which are the key variables? How much impact does a change in them have on sales? What are the main assumptions and what do they rest on? Could they change? To better understand your market and your model, it's helpful to create and test various scenarios, as we discuss below.

Summary of key concepts

- **Volume**: widgets, meals, projects, hours, etc. Measured in units.

- **Value**: money, measured in currency.

- **Installed base**: the total of all units installed or present in the market since sales began; a "stock".

- **Annual sales**: the volume of sales in a given year; a "flow".

- **Penetration**: the total of your installed base as a percentage of the total market installed based.

- **Market share**: your annual sales as a percentage of total market sales in a specific year.

- **Garbage in, Garbage out**: ensure that your data is as accurate as possible and that your assumptions are reasonable.

- **Assumptions**: make your assumptions explicit; a forecasting model is not a black box.

- **Understanding market dynamics**: don't focus solely on your model's output; you can also use your model to better understand your market's dynamics.

PART II:

What to consider before you begin

A s with many things, people are often tempted to fire up their spreadsheet and immediately start building a sales forecasting model before they've carefully consi-dered all the parameters. It's wiser to consider several important issues before you actually start to build any model or make your forecast.

Define your market

One of the first questions you should ask is: "how do I define my market?" Where will you draw the line?

Some questions to consider are:

• What types of consumers does your market include? Is it all consumers or are you serving a niche or sub-culture? Can you identify each sub-segment of the market?

• Which product categories does your market cover?

• Where's the boundary of your market? Which activities of the value chain does it include (design, production, distri-bution, retailing, etc.)? Are you forward and backward integrated or focused on just one small part of the value chain (e.g. just distribution)?

Carefully defining your market is important for several rea-sons. First of all, if you define your market too narrowly, you may get blindsided by new competitors whom you didn't even realize existed. Imagine, for example, that you define your market as soft drinks. Suddenly, however, new competitors emerge who sell sports drinks, healthy drinks, etc. These products begin to eat away at your market share. Why? Because the consumer is only really interested in function (note: we ignore the role of brand here), which in this case could be taste, convenience, healthiness or a caffeine jolt (performance). Moreover, consumer tastes may have changed or new consumer segments may have emerged. The market then is really "all liquid refreshment", and you probably should have defined it as such. Obviously, it's a much bigger market. You may need to forecast your sales in the context of this much larger market. On the other hand, sometimes it's wise to forecast sub-segments of the market while considering the overall whole in order to avoid losing focus.

Soft drinks vs. Beverages

* All brands shown are the trademarks of their respective owners.

Extrapolate or not?

Another thing to consider is: "can I extrapolate from the present or not?" If your industry is stable and sales tend to follow a predictable pattern, then extrapolation is a viable forecasting method. If, on the other hand, your industry is subject to disruptive change, then the present will not be a good predictor of the future. In this case, it may be virtually impossible to extrapolate from the present. You will need to select the most appropriate forecasting technique accordingly.

Market characteristics

Before you embark on building your sales forecast, it is wise to consider the characteristics of your market. This will improve the quality of your insights and assumptions.

Here are some points to consider:

- **Seasonality**: is your industry subject to seasonality? Think of the fashion, retail, or tourism industries; they're very seasonal. The summer and winter seasons tend to be the peak seasons in the tourism industry (depending upon location and/or type of leisure activities offered) whereas the end of the year is usually the most important period in the retail industry. Seasonality makes your sales "lumpy" or uneven over the course of a year.

- **Market size**: what is the overall market size? You need to know how big the sandbox is in which you are playing. How big are your sales relative to the total market? What is a realistic market share, given the size of the overall market? It is usually easier to grab a relatively small share in a big market (with many small competitors) than in a small market (dominated by only a few large competitors).

- **Market growth**: how fast is the market growing? What is the annual rate of sales growth? Generally speaking, it is easier to grow your sales in a growing market than in a flat or declining market.

- **Market stage**: at what stage of development is your market? Similar to the growth rate, this suggests how much growth you could reasonably expect. Obviously, it's usually more difficult to grab market share in a mature or declining market (unless many competitors are exiting the market and you have a competitive advantage, of course).

- **Competition**: are there many competitors or just a few? Is the market a monopoly or oligopoly? The degree of competition will impact your ability to grow your sales, maintain your market share and raise or sustain your price level.

- **Price development**: how will your price evolve relative to the prices of your competitors? Will you have a price advantage? Will there be downward pressure on prices? Price competition can affect both the volume and value of your sales, impacting the latter directly.

- **Technology**: are there any new or improved technologies on the horizon that could completely change the game?

- **Consumption**: what about consumers? Will there be completely different consumption patterns? Will consumer tastes change? Think of all the new gadgets that are very popular now. These consumer "needs" did not even exist 20-30 years ago.

- **Regulatory environment**: nearly every industry is subject to some degree of regulation, while some are highly regulated. New regulation can change the game in one fell swoop.

Summary of key concepts

- **Define your market**: which market segments does it include? Which activities in the value chain does it cover? Properly defining your market helps you to be aware of potential sources of competition as well as to identify latent or new consumer tastes.

- **Extrapolate or not**: if your market is stable and predictable, you may be able to extrapolate from current sales; if your market is subject to disruptive change, it may be wiser not to extrapolate.

- **Market characteristics**: consider the key characteristics of your market before you start building your forecast. This will improve the quality of your insights and assumptions.

PART III:

16 Easy and Effective Sales Forecasting Techniques

Here are 16 easy and effective sales forecasting techniques. They are easy and quick to learn and apply. You don't need to know any complex statistical methods or how to use any software beyond Microsoft® Excel* or another spreadsheet program. The techniques are effective because they are proven and straightforward – we don't over-complicate things here. Remember, however, that ultimately the accuracy and usefulness of your forecast will depend on the assumptions you make, the logic you use to construct your model and the data you feed into it.

This list is fairly comprehensive, but if you discover another technique not included here that you think could be effective, by all means try it out. You may also contact me at www.salesforecasting.biz to see what I think of it. If I consider it useful, I'll include it in a future update of this guide.

Let's get started. For each technique I'm going to tell you when to use it, how to use it and usually I'll give one or more examples.

The table below provides an overview of all 16 sales forecasting techniques:

---

* Microsoft Excel is a trademark of the Microsoft Corporation.

Technique	When to use it	What to watch out for
Technique #1: Ask your sales force	Prospective customers can easily be identified	Manipulation of data by sales people to serve their own purposes
Technique #2: Conduct a market survey	It's relatively easy to acquire accurate data from customers or channel partners	• Requires cooperation of customers or channel partners • Need to receive accurate data on time
Technique #3: Expert Panel (Delphi)	The opinion of knowledgeable and unbiased market experts is available	• Ensure that experts are unbiased • Avoid groupthink
Technique #4: Extrapolate – historical growth rate	Market is stable, mature and relatively predictable	• Doesn't take into account seasonality • Depends on accuracy of the growth rate that you predict/assume
Technique #5: Extrapolate – "Run Rate"	To forecast sales thru the end of the period in a predictable market	Does not account for seasonality
Technique #6: Extrapolate - Moving Average	To increase accuracy of forecast in a relatively stable market	Availability of historical/actual data
Technique #7: Extrapolate – Trend-fitting	Fast and effective extrapolation	Availability of historical/actual data
Technique #8: Leading Indicators	Leading indicators exist or can be constructed, and their relationship to sales is well-defined	Be aware of time lags

Technique	When to use it	What to watch out for
Technique #9: Apply Ratios	Variables that drive business exist and can be captured in ratios	Avoid over-averaging
Technique #10: Modeling	Can apply growth pattern from similar product or service	Ensure that product or service is really comparable, or adjust the growth rate accordingly
Technique #11: Growth Pattern-fitting	New product introductions or products that follow an identifiable evolution	Clearly identify the major inflection points and a realistic timeframe for the pattern
Technique #12: Share of	You know total market size or spending	• Drill down to the right level • Don't over-simplify
Technique #13: Maximum Penetration	You know total market size or spending and can assume growth to a steady state	A static measure
Technique #14 Replacement Rate	For existing markets	Assumes customer purchases are spread out evenly over time (or you adjust for different patterns)
Technique #15: Price Elasticity	Price-Volume relationship can be measured or applied from other products or services	Measured relationship can be reasonably applied to your product or service
Technique #16: Rolling Forecast	To increase forecast accuracy when faced with rapidly evolving market or internal operations	• Frequent revisions to forecast may make people complacent and reduces credibility of forecast • Constant adjustments to sales targets confuses • Commitment of time and resources

Technique #1: Ask your sales force

Sticking with the KISS philosophy, this technique is very simple, yet highly effective. You can use it when you have what I call "named accounts" – when you can actually identify each of your prospective customers by name.

This technique is often used for B2B high-value products or services for which you have a relatively small number of prospective customers whom it is thus easy to identify. Examples would be turbines, power plants, jumbo jets, enterprise IT or CT scanners to name but a few. As you can see, all of these are large ticket items. The main point is that you can identify your customers or customer organization individually. Thus, the technique need not necessarily be limited to B2B high-value products or services. A small business could also use this technique, assuming the scale of its market is limited. Imagine a local gourmet food shop, for example. The owner could easily identify businesses, households or individual consumers within a certain limited radius who need her products or services.

• • •

Caution

When using this technique, you need to be careful with your sales people. No offense is meant towards sales people, but the reality is that most sales people are motivated by their bonus, as they should be. Therefore, they may have an incentive to artificially deflate or inflate the market in order to more easily achieve their sales targets and thereby get their bonus. Just keep that in mind when you receive data from them. On the other hand, sales people are a very rich resource because they are so close to the market. If they're any good, they should be in contact with actual or potential customers and know what their future spending plans are.

How to use it:

Your account managers should be able to provide you with the name of the account, when to expect a purchase, the size of the budget and maybe even the configuration or type of product or service – what the customer is going to want in a little more detail – as well as the likely competitors.

You could also use the lifetime of products that the customer currently has to calculate the replacement rate and thereby have a rough idea of when a customer would need to purchase a new product. We discuss this in detail below. In a nutshell, if you know that you've sold a system at a certain customer, and you know that your system has an average lifespan of 10 years, then you know that they'll be replacing your system in 10 years (hopefully with a system that's again from you). That means that the account will be up for grabs again in 10 years. Knowing the likely timing of the account's next purchase, you can include them in your forecast.

Technique #2: Conduct a market survey

The survey technique is also fairly simple but can be effective. Use it when you have very cooperative and knowledgeable customers or channel partners. They probably should be a relatively small and easy to identify group of buyers. Moreover, the data they provide you with should reflect the entire market. It doesn't mean that the data you collect necessarily has to cover the entire market. You might be able to extrapolate or infer the size and growth of the entire market based on a subset of data – the smaller set of data that you collect. You might collect data that covers 80% of the market, for example, and extrapolate the remaining 20%. The point is that whatever data you collect should give you an accurate picture of the total market.

• • •

Caution

Obviously, the data you collect should be accurate, and it should also be relatively easy to collect the data. For this, you depend upon your customers or channel partners.

• • •

How to use it:

You would conduct an annual, quarterly or monthly survey of your customers and/or channel partners on their purchase or sales expectations. Be sure to give them clear instructions or even a template (e.g. in MS-Excel) for data collection. Ideally, make the data collected in the template easy to map to your sales forecasting model so that you don't run into definition problems or have to re-calculate data. Speaking of definitions: make sure that you use consistent definitions throughout and that your customers or channel partners understand and apply the same definitions.

More sophisticated companies and those with the budget may want to automate some or all of the data collection process (the same recommendations regarding consistency and definitions would apply – in fact, they probably take on even greater importance when the process is automated). Then data could be easily collected and fed directly into your model (perhaps after validation or "cleaning"). If you do automate the data collection process, try to ensure that it does not become overly rigid. I recommend leaving yourself the flexibility to make some changes to your forecasting model without having to completely re-architect and re-build your data collection system.

● ● ●
Keep Track

As an added measure of security, you might want to track your customers' or channel partners' expectations against actual sales performance in order to judge the reliability of what they say over time. Do they often say they're going to purchase 100 and then only purchase 80?

● ● ●

Technique #3: Expert Panel (Delphi)

You can use this technique when the opinion or knowledge of (hopefully) unbiased experts is available. Ideally, you would need three or more experts.

● ● ●

Caution

You're fully dependent on the objectivity of the experts. Be careful that you don't have an expert who is biased or has a conflict of interest or other hidden agenda.

● ● ●

How to use it:

Ask the experts to write down their forecasts. They should not see each other's forecasts at this point nor should they discuss them amongst themselves; each expert should arrive at his or her forecast independently.

Next, share the forecasts amongst all the experts. Then give the experts the chance to revise their forecasts based upon the forecasts of the other experts.

What you'll notice is that often the forecasts will converge towards a consensus view. This consensus view will often be more accurate than any one expert's view would have been.

• • •

 Caution

Ensure that each expert arrives at his or her initial forecast independently or else you risk "group think".

Expert panels: It's just common sense!

When I was studying for my MBA at London Business School, I remember sitting in a finance class. The professor was presenting the various valuations calculated by different people for a mine (it was the Bula Mines case). The professor spent one hour describing the relative merits of each valuation, focusing on the intricacies of valuation using net present value.

The guy sitting next to me was a spacey kid from Denver, Colorado who had this kind of Western drawl like a cowboy. Well, half way through our professor's lengthy dissertation, this kid leans over to me and whispers in my ear that the correct answer is probably just the average of all the experts' different views.

I remember thinking to myself: "Well, what does he know? He's just a space cowboy!" But to my astonishment, a few minutes later when the professor revealed the "correct" answer it was pretty much just what the "Colorado Kid" had predicted. Now, I'm certainly not advocating against the use of techniques like net present value, my only point is that expert panels can and do work.

Technique #4: Extrapolate – historical growth rate

There are several forecasting techniques that are related as they are all based on extrapolation. Technique four is to use an historical growth rate. This technique is exceedingly simple, but if it works, why not use it?

One pre-requisite is that you're participating in a stable, mature market and probably your market share is relatively stable with a degree of predictability.

• • •

 Caution

• This technique does not take into account seasonality.

• This technique depends wholly upon the accuracy of the growth rate that you predict/assume.

• • •

How to use it:

Apply a growth rate from previous periods, which could be months, quarters or years. Let's say that you want to predict next year's sales. You know this year's sales. You would multiply this year's actual sales by one plus an annual rate of sales growth, which you assume. Another way of saying the same thing is that to predict next year's sales growth you would take this year's actual sales plus the increase in annual sales, in terms of volume or value, not the percentage growth rate. These are two different ways of calculating sales but they are basically the same and yield the same result.

Key formulas:

• Next year's sales = This year's sales x (1 + % rate of sales growth)

Next year's sales = This year's sales + increase in annual sales

Personally, I find the first method is somehow faster because you save a conceptual step. As I've said, however, both methods yield the same result.

Examples:

Next year's sales = This year's sales x (1 + % rate of sales growth)

$$= \$100 \times (1 + 10\%)$$

$$= \$110$$

Next year's sales = This year's sales + increase in sales

$$= \$100 + (\$100 \times 10\%)$$

$$= \$100 + \$10$$

$$= \$110$$

Technique #5: Extrapolate – "Run Rate"

Another way to extrapolate is to use a "run rate". A run rate is an average calculated from past historical periods (i.e. using actual rather than forecast data).

You can use a run-rate for stable, mature markets that have a relatively high degree of predictability. A run rate is often used to forecast sales through the end of the period.

• • •

 Caution

This technique does not account for seasonality.

• • •

How to use it:

Calculate and apply a "run-rate" or average of sales for the period. To do so, divide the year-to-date sales by the number of sales periods to date. Now multiply this run-rate that you've calculated by the number of remaining sales periods and add it to your year-to-date sales.

Key formulas:

- **Run rate** = Total revenue-to-date / # of sales periods-to-date

- **Projected annual sales** = Total revenue-to-date + (Run rate x Remaining # of sales periods)

Example:

You've done $300 sales in the first quarter. So your year-to-date sales are $300. Your monthly run rate is then $300/3 months = $100/month. On average, you've been booking sales of $100 per month. There are nine months left in the year so you multiply your run rate of $100/month by nine months, giving you forecast or estimated sales for the remainder of the period of $900. Add $900 to $300 to get the estimated or forecast annual sales of $1,200.

Technique #6: Extrapolate - Moving Average

You can use this technique under the same circumstances as techniques four and five. The only caveat is that you need sales data for multiple historical periods. Taking a moving average over several periods helps to increase the accuracy of your forecast.

How to use it:

Add up sales for the most recent period, for example three years. Divide this sum by the number of periods to calculate the moving average. This average is then the forecast for the next period. This sounds a lot like run-rate and it's indeed similar, but the difference is that it's *moving*. Your average is a "window" (for example, of three months) that shifts forward each time your actual sales move to the next period.

Example:

We have actual sales for years one through five and we want to forecast sales for year six. Column two lists our sales volume while column three lists our cumulative three-year sales total. The fourth column shows the three-year moving average, which is that year's 3-year cumulative sales total divided by three.

The moving average in year three is 340. That's the sum of 300 + 350 + 370, which gives the three-year sales total of 1,020, divided by three periods to yield the three-year moving average of 340. The process is repeated for year four. The only difference is that since we want to calculate the moving average, we shift everything forward by one year. Now we add up 350 (the sales for year 2), 370 (the sales for year 3) and 330 (the sales for year 4). This yields a total of 1,050 (the three-year sales total). Dividing this by three yields a 3-year moving average of 350. In year five, we'd have a three-year moving average of 367, which would be the forecast sales for year six.

Year	Sales Volume	3-Year Sales Total	3-Year Moving Average
1	300		
2	350		
3	370	1,020	340
4	330	1,050	350
5	400	1,100	**367**
6E	**367**		

Technique #7: Extrapolate – Trend-fitting

The last of the extrapolation techniques is trend fitting. I like trend fitting because it's so easy. Having said that, its very simplicity creates the danger that you apply it in a rote, overly-simplistic way.

You can use it in the same circumstances as the other extrapolation techniques. You must, however, have sales data for multiple historical periods.

How to use it:

Let's say that you've got some historical data and you want to fit a trend line to that data.

You could "eyeball" it, just making an educated guess as to estimated sales in future periods based on what would seem to fit your past data. That, however, is probably neither the best way nor the easiest way to estimate the trend. Instead, you can use a tool such as MS-Excel. Excel is incredibly easy to use and very fast once you know how to use it. The TREND and FORECAST functions can be used in a spreadsheet table or you can simply add a trend line to your charted data. In my opinion, the latter option is the easiest. The extension of the trend line is then your forecast.

Imagine that you have sales over five years. Using the TREND or FORECAST function you could easily forecast sales for years six and seven inside your spreadsheet table. As noted above, however, it's much easier to just add a trend line to a chart. Start by charting or plotting your data. Next, click on one of your data points to select that series of data. Right click on your mouse and select "Add Trendline" to show a window that gives you various options. Select the type of trend line that you want to fit: linear, logarithmic, etc. Most of the time, a linear trend line will do, although it depends upon your sales data. If your sales data is all over the map, then one of the other types of trend line may fit it better.

To forecast: click on the options tab and select the number of periods ahead that you want to forecast. I recommend also selecting "Display equation on chart". That way you'll be able to calculate the actual forecast numbers as opposed to guessing them from the chart. By plugging a few numbers into the equation (the forecast periods), you'll be able to calculate the actual forecast numbers. You can also select "Display R-squared value on chart". The R-squared value describes how well your trend line fits your data so the higher the percentage the better (note: this is the only time in this book that I talk about statistics!).

In the example below, you plug values into the equation to calculate the actual sales numbers. Y would be the sales, X is the year. To get year 6 sales we'd plug in 6 so it would be 19 x 6 + 87 = 201.

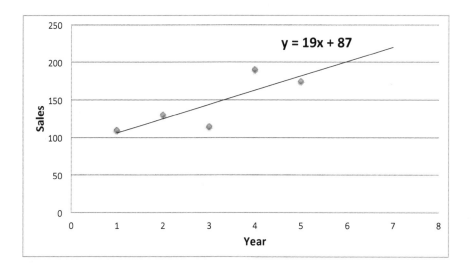

Technique #8: Leading Indicators

What is a leading indicator? You've probably heard the term used by economists because they tend to use leading indicators such as economic sentiment, housing starts, or inventories in their forecasts.

For our purposes, leading indicators are variables that change in advance of and can be used to predict sales.

You can use this technique, first of all, when leading indicators actually exist (or you are able to construct your own). The relationship between leading indicator and sales must also be well defined. You need to understand this relationship; it should be very clear and transparent. As discussed above, forecasting should not be a black box.

How to use it

Identify one or more leading indicators. Next, clarify as precisely as possible the relationship between the indicators and sales. You might find, for example, that when a particular leading indicator grows by one percent your sales grow by five percent, with a three-month lag. There will normally be a time lag so it's important to understand the timing as well.

Example:

This is real data from the semiconductor industry. The book-to-bill ratio is the value of sales booked or orders received divided by the value of sales that have actually been shipped and invoiced, the billings. A book-to-bill ratio greater than one means that orders exceed billings and sales are likely to increase. In other words, there is pent up or unfulfilled demand.

| | Bookings | Billings | Book-to-Bill |
	(3-Month avg.)	(3-Month avg.)	Ratio
Jul-14	$1,413.7	$1,317.6	1.07
Jun-14	$1,455.0	$1,327.5	1.10
May-14	$1,407.0	$1,407.8	1.00
Apr-14	$1,443.0	$1,403.2	1.03
Mar-14	$1,297.7	$1,225.5	1.06
Feb-14	$1,295.4	$1,288.3	1.01
Jan-14	$1,280.3	$1,233.2	1.04

Technique #9: Apply Ratios

This is one of my favorite sales forecasting techniques, not only because it's relatively easy to apply, but also because it forces you to understand the main drivers of your market.

Use this technique when there are identifiable variables that drive your business and these variables can be captured in ratios. Some examples are the conversion rate for online or web sales, or sales per square foot or square meter in the retail industry. Some industries have very specific metrics. The airline industry, for example, uses load factor (a measure of capacity utilization) and revenue passenger miles or kilometers (a measure of value generated per amount of capacity).

• • •

Caution

Ratios are relatively easy to use and they capture the key relationships, but there's a danger of over-averaging or over-simplifying. Despite what I said about KISS, you don't want to go to an extreme and over-simplify. That could be the "kiss" of death!

• • •

How to use it:

Determine the key ratio or metric for your industry. Either it's well known or standard in your industry or you can devise one yourself. Use this ratio to calculate sales. To avoid over-averaging, you may need to forecast different market segments separately. Remember: every industry calculation will be different.

Example 1:

Suppose you have an online business selling e-books. You could start by estimating your traffic. Let's say that you expect 10,000 visitors per month. Another assumption would be that of those 10,000 visitors, 10% click through to your sales page. Actually, it's not necessarily an assumption since it might be based on statistics from your actual web traffic data. In any case, that's 1,000 visitors. Of those, 5% are converted and actually buy something. That's 50 people. Let's assume that each of these 50 customers spends, on average, £100. That gives you 50 customers x £100 = £5,000/month of revenue.

Example 2:

Now suppose that you own a small retail shop that has peak and off-peak selling hours. In order to avoid the problem of over-averaging, you could forecast two streams of revenue separately. Here we'll use sales per square meter (foot) per hour. During peak selling times the sales per square meter are £500 per square meter, whereas during non-peak selling times they are £100. What you could do is to break the hours down into peak hours in one week. So peak hours, such as weekends and lunch times, during a single week amount to 20 hours. Non-peak hours amount to 30 hours.

To calculate sales, take sales per square meter per hour times the number of hours times the total floor space. In the peak case, this would be £20 per square meter per hour times 20 hours times 100 square meters. That would give you sales of £40,000. During off-peak times, sales are only £5 per square meter per hour times 30 hours times 100 square meters, giving you sales of £15,000. That means that your weekly sales are £40,000 (the sales during peak hours), plus £15,000 (the sales during off-peak hours), or £55,000.

One thing you might want to do additionally, if appropriate, is to adjust for seasonality or any holidays when the store might be closed or it might be open and there might be more peak times.

As you can see, it's sometimes important to split things into a finer level of granularity in order to avoid over-averaging.

Key Formulas:

- Sales/m^2/hour x # of hours x floor space available
- Peak hours: £20/m^2/hour x 20 hours x 100m^2 = £40,000
- Non-peak hours: £5/m^2/hour x 30 hours x 100m^2 = £15,000
- Weekly sales: £40,000 + £15,000 = £55,000

Technique #10: Modeling

This is an easy technique to use but needs to be used with caution. You would use this when you have a similar growth rate or pattern that you can apply. It might be from a product that has attributes which are similar to those of your product's, or which serves a similar market segment. This technique is often very useful for forecasting sales from new product introductions since in such cases you usually don't really know how sales will develop but you can apply the patterns from the past experience of similar products to your new product.

How to use it:

Simply apply the growth rate from a comparable product or service to the one for which you're creating a forecast. You could apply a single rate for the entire forecast horizon, or you could break it down into discrete periods or phases. What you could also do, if you have the budget, resources and time, is to run a test market on a narrower geographical area or segment and then apply the growth rate that you get to forecast the overall market. This assumes, of course, that it's reasonable to extrapolate from the test market to the overall market.

Example:

You're an apparel company and you're going to launch a new jacket style that targets young urban professionals. You have no idea how this new jacket style is going to be received by the market, but you do know that a similar jacket style in previous years sold 100 units in its first year and then grew by 5% every year thereafter. Given fashion trends, after three years, sales growth flattened. You could apply the figures from this other product – which you think is similar to the product that you're going to be selling – to forecast sales. Take an average price, say, $20. You're confident that the market is going to grow at 5% per annum as in the case of the other product. Moreover, you're fairly certain that you'll be able to sell 100 units in the first year and that sales will grow by 5% in year two to 105, and then again by 5% in year three to 110. In year four, growth will start to flatten and in year five it will stay flat. Apply the average price to your unit sales to calculate revenue.

• • •

Caution:

The modeling technique is simple but can be highly effective, provided that you identify a product or service that is actually similar to the one for which you are making a forecast. You may need to tweak the rates of growth, however, to better fit your product.

• • •

Technique #11: Growth Pattern-fitting

This technique is very useful for new product introductions and for products that typically follow a certain evolution.

• • •

 Caution:

You really need to pay attention to the timing of the growth pattern, how it will change over time and inflection points, if there are any. At what point will growth accelerate or decelerate? When will it change in a major way? When will it go up or go down?

• • •

How to use it:

Decide on the pattern or shape that best fits your offering (this technique could actually be called "shape-fitting"). That could be a classic S-curve; an exponential curve in which growth is slow in the beginning and then suddenly shoots up; fast growth to maturity; or growth that is fast but then slows until you offer an upgrade or next generation product and then growth picks up again; it could be a fad in which sales grow suddenly and precipitously but then drop off in an equally precipitous way; or it could be seasonal such that it has peaks and troughs.

As mentioned above, the important thing is to decide on the time frame for the entire curve and identify any inflection points. Inflection points are where growth will change in a major

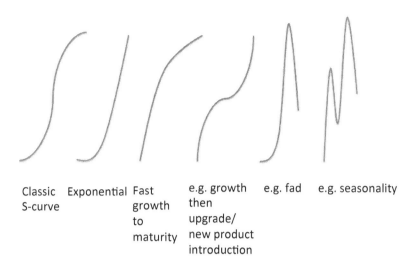

| Classic S-curve | Exponential | Fast growth to maturity | e.g. growth then upgrade/ new product introduction | e.g. fad | e.g. seasonality |

way – it may shoot up or it may crash; there will be a major change in the shape of the curve.

Here's where you could go against my KISS principle and use a mathematical formula because each of these growth curves has a mathematical formula associated with it. Even if you did that, however (and I don't necessarily advise you to do so), you'd still need to adjust your results because a mathematical formula may not properly reflect the reality of the market. Just plugging numbers blindly into a formula is probably not what you're paid to do; you're probably paid to use your brain and think whether this really fits your market. In other words, you need to interpret your model.

What you could also do is to identify the type of growth pattern or shape of curve, and then simply "eyeball it" and put in rates of growth or units that roughly follow the shape of the curve, based on your view of how sales are likely to develop. Remember: this is not rocket science. This is part "art", not just "science". So, your "best guess" is often just that: the best guess.

If you happen to have historical data from a similar case, you could also simply fit a trend line to it, as we've seen earlier. That would give you a pretty good indication of the rates of growth to use in making your forecast. Don't rely on automatic mechanisms, however. You need to always interpret data and decide for yourself whether they make sense.

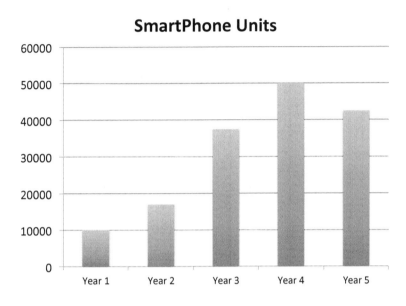

Here's an example where I've simply eyeballed the pattern curve and put in units that made sense to me. Let's suppose we're about to introduce a new smartphone. Suppose the typical lifetime of a smartphone is five years: after five years, sales start to flatten or drop off. Based on experience, we know that annual sales could be 10,000 units in the first year and 50,000 units in year four. Moreover, we know that sales usually follow some kind of S-curve. Here I've simply put in these numbers. You could argue whether it's going to be 20,000 units in year two or 25,000 or 18,000. In a sense, those are fine differences. The important thing is that you know that sales of the new smartphone are going to follow an S-curve evolution. And you know that the starting point is likely to be around 10,000 units and the ending point is likely to be around 50,000, before the market starts to decline.

Technique #12: Share of

I find this technique to be quite useful but also dangerous when overused or misused. You can use it for pretty much anything: any product or service whether it's B2B or B2C. As long as you know the total spending or total market size, or can estimate them, you can use "share of".

• • •

 Caution

Make sure that you drill down to the market in which you'll actually be competing. As discussed above, you need to pay attention to how to define your market or where you draw the boundary for your industry. It's important that you define your market narrowly enough so that you can accurately forecast it.

The biggest danger when using this technique is that you over-simplify; you may be tempted to simply pluck a number out of thin air. Remember that there's competition, there are obstacles; any number of factors could reduce your sales.

• • •

How to use it:

Estimate the total spending or market size. This is your point of reference. Then estimate your share of it: what you think would be a reasonable share of that market that you could grab.

Example:

As an example, let's take the electronic medical record (EMR) business. It's a $20 billion business in the US. Suppose that it's expected to grow by 10% per annum over the next 10 years. We know that there are five major competitors, that they control 80% of the market, and that the market leader has a 20% share. Imagine that our company is a new entrant. Realistically we don't expect to be able to grab 15% of the market in the first year, but we do think we could achieve a 1% market share – because we're already active in a related segment – and grow to a 5% market share because we're putting a lot of resources into advertising, relationship building, and other marketing acti-vities. That may be reasonable but you must be able to justify your assumptions, particularly with this technique.

Here you see our market share increasing. The market is growing by 10% every year over five years. By multiplying our market share of one percent (growing to five percent) by the total size of the market we get our annual revenue.

('000s)	Year 1	Year 2	Year 3	Year 4	Year 5
Total market annual sales	20,000	22,000	24,200	26,620	29,282
Our market share	1%	2%	3%	4%	5%
Our EMR's revenue	200	440	726	1,065	1,464

Technique #13: Maximum Penetration

Technique #13 is similar to technique #12 in a conceptual sense. You can use it when you assume that the market will grow to saturation and reach a steady state, and when you know the total market size. Unlike with "share of", however, with maximum penetration, you tend to measure sales by penetration rate and not by value. You can use maximum penetration either for forecasting the total market size each year and/or for forecasting your own annual market share.

How to use it:

First, identify the market. Then determine the likely maximum penetration: what is the percentage of the market that you think will ultimately be using this product or service? Also ask yourself how many years you think it will take to reach that maximum penetration. Then decide what the rate of growth would be until you reach that steady state or maximum penetration.

• • •

Caution:

This is a fairly static measure since you assume fairly steady growth to a maximum.

• • •

Example:

Imagine that you're forecasting the market for in-home solar power systems. You can assume then that the market is "all households". Let's say that there are one million households. We think that 90% of them will have solar power by the year 2020 whereas only 10% of them currently have solar. We're pretty sure that growth will follow the classic S-curve, perhaps without a decline in the market so much as growth simply leveling off to a steady state.

We also believe that our annual market share will be stable and track the market at 10%. Taking an average spending per household or an average price per system, we can calculate our sales revenue. We might include what I call "replacement rate" in our calculation (see below). Assume that the market reaches a maximum penetration and then every few years a family replaces their system such that the market continues on ad infinitum in a steady state.

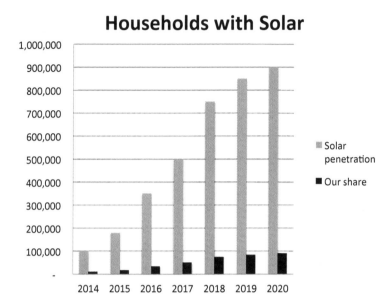

Technique #14 Replacement Rate

You can't really use this technique to forecast new markets but it can be highly useful for forecasting existing markets. It involves estimating potential sales based on replacement purchases.

This technique works for any product that has a defined lifetime – whether it's a large industrial machine or a kitchen appliance. You could possibly apply it to services if the service is consumed on a regular basis and the frequency of its consumption is known. The replacement rate technique is strictly for use in forecasting existing markets; it doesn't take into account completely new purchases, i.e. purchases by customers who have never purchased the product from you or your competition. The replacement rate technique could be used, however, to forecast purchases by customers switching to your brand from a competitor's brand.

The starting point is to estimate the lifetime of the product.

Let's suppose that the lifetime of this product is 10 years. You can then infer that on average every year 10% of the installed base is replaced. In other words, the replacement rate is 10%. So the annual replacement market size would be equal to the replacement rate times the size of the installed base times an average price.

You might actually break down the market into several segments and perform the calculation for each segment separately. This might be necessitated by the fact that your products have different lifetimes. It helps you to make a calculation that's much more accurate. You might also apply *Technique #12: Share of* to estimate how much of the replacement market you could grab.

Key formulas:

- Annual Replacement Market (units) = Replacement rate x Installed base

- Annual Replacement Market (value) = Replacement rate x Installed base x Average price

Example:

Suppose you're forecasting sales of a universal power supply that has a lifetime of five years. Since consumers replace their systems every five years, on average in any given year 20% of consumers will be replacing their systems. That means that the replacement rate is one divided by five or 20%. Let's suppose that the total installed base is equal to one million units. To calculate the number of units being replaced each year, multiply the replacement rate of 20% by one million units; every year 200,000 units are being replaced. Let's suppose that the average price of a system is $1,000. Multiplying annual unit sales of 200,000 units times the average price of $1,000/unit gives annual sales of $200 million. Assuming that our share of that could be 5%, then 5% of $200 million is equivalent to $10 million. That would be our annual sales in the replacement market. Remember it doesn't necessarily include completely new sales (see "caution" below). It's exclusively sales among existing UPS users.

- Universal Power Supply (UPS) has a lifetime of 5 years
- Replacement rate = 1 ÷ 5 = 20%
- Total installed base = 1 million units
- 20% x 1 million units = 200,000 units replaced each year
- Average price = $1,000/unit
- 200,000 units x $1,000/unit = $200 million
- Our share = 5% of $200 million = $10 million

• • •

Caution:

It should be pointed out that one massive assumption with this technique is that not every customer organization has purchased their product at the same time or in the same year. Purchases have been evenly spread out over time such that products will not reach their end-of-life all in the same year.

Of course, if you know the pattern of purchases (e.g. 50% were made in the first year and then 10% every year for five years thereafter) and the total period of the pattern (e.g. the purchase pattern runs for six years and then repeats itself) then you could apply that pattern instead of the pattern presented above in which consumers replace the same percentage of systems every year).

• • •

	Year 1	Year 2	Year 3	Year 4	Year 5	Year 6
Smooth purchase pattern	20%	20%	20%	20%	20%	20%
Uneven purchase pattern	50%	10%	10%	10%	10%	10%

Technique #15: Price Elasticity

This technique is somewhat complicated and thus should only be used in very specific circumstances.

For those who don't have a background in economics, the idea behind price elasticity is that a relatively small change in price results in a disproportionately large change in the quantity of your product or service demanded. When your product is price elastic, if you reduce its price even just a little, the quantity of your product demanded will increase much more. In other words, the market is very sensitive to price. On the other hand, your product is price inelastic when demand is not sensitive to price. In this case, even if you reduce your price, consumers will not demand disproportionately more of your product.

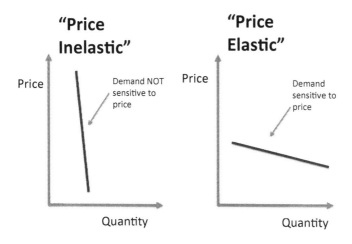

The idea with price elasticity in a business context is that you can actually increase your overall revenue. The easiest way to understand these concepts – and their impact on revenue – is through an example.

Example:

Imagine that you have a product priced at $10 per unit. At that price the market demands 100 units. Your revenue, therefore, is $10 x 100 units = $1,000.

Now, let's suppose that consumers are price sensitive, the product is price elastic. By lowering your price, you'll lose revenue because of the fact that you now charge less per unit. This loss in revenue, however, will be more than compensated for by an increase in volume. In other words, when you lower your price, the decrease in revenue due to the lower price will be more than offset by the increase in revenue due to the increased quantity of your product demanded by consumers. You'll gain so much more in unit sales that the overall effect on revenue will be positive.

For example, if you lower your price from $10 to $8, then your total revenue will increase because now instead of selling 100 units, you actually triple your unit sales to 300 units, and $8 times 300 is $2,400 in revenue. This is more than double your previous revenue of $1,000.

• • •

Caution:

To use price elasticity to forecast sales, you need reliable data. In theory, this technique works for any product or service, but you need to be sure that your product or service exhibits a price sensitivity that is similar to the price sensitivity of the product for which you measured price sensitivity. Suppose that you measured price sensitivity or price elasticity for product A and now you're forecasting sales for product B. You want to be sure that the same price quantity demand relationship that applied to product A will apply to product B.

• • •

How to use it:

Calculate price elasticity for one or several products or services, and ideally over a range of prices and quantities so that you can identify different elasticities and relationships. Take the average or the relationship that you conclude is most probable and apply that calculated price elasticity to your product or service.

Example:

Suppose you have the following data:

- Price ranges from $8 up to $12.
- Quantity demanded ranges from 180 units down to 70 units.

Price	Quantity Demanded
12	70
11	90
10	100
9	130
8	180

Let's calculate the price elasticity between a price of $10 and $9 and a quantity demanded of 100 and 130. To do so, we'll take the percentage change in the quantity demanded divided by the percentage change in price.

To calculate the percentage change in the quantity demanded:

(100-130)/100 = -0.3 or 30%

We ignore the minus sign because we assume that the following relationship exists: that when price goes down, quantity demanded goes up.

Then we do the same thing for price. We calculate the percentage change in price.

($10-$9)/$10 = -0.1 or 10%.

Dividing 0.3 by 0.1 yields a price elasticity of three.

If price elasticity is three, it means that a 10% reduction in price will lead to a 30% increase in the quantity demanded.

• • •

 Caution:

Be careful. Measured price elasticity can vary widely depending upon how you measured it, for which products, and where on the demand curve.

• • •

Technique #16: Rolling Forecast

Remember *Technique #6: Extrapolate - Moving Average*? A rolling forecast is a similar forecasting technique. You also apply a moving time window but you don't apply an average. A rolling forecast is useful when you're faced with a market or internal operations that are rapidly evolving.

How to use it:

The number of periods in a rolling forecast remains constant, but you shift the forecast period (or "window") forward as each new period begins. For a 12-month forecast, for example, you would add the new month and drop out the last old month such that you always maintain a current 12-month forecast. The advantage with a rolling forecast is that you more frequently (in this example, each month) reassess your forecast based on developments in the market and actual sales instead of attempting to forecast for a longer period and only reassessing your forecast after a longer interval (e.g. quarterly or annually, in the case of our example).

A rolling forecast also gives you the chance to see how good your original forecast was:

- **Period that drops out of the forecast window**: assess forecast sales for the period that drops out of the forecast window against actual sales. How large is the variance (the difference between the actual and forecast sales)? In the example below, when the forecast window shifts ahead by one month to the April-March period, for the just completed month of March we could then compare forecast sales with actual sales.

- **Periods that were previously forecast**: for each month, compare your previous forecast with your new forecast. In the example below, when the forecast window shifts ahead by one month to the April-March period, we could compare the old forecasts for each month from April-February with the new forecasts. Are there large differences? What accounts for the large differences? Were there unforeseen changes in the market or your business or is there a deficiency in your forecasting method?

Mar	Apr	May	Jun	Jul	Aug	Sep	Oct	Nov	Dec	Jan	Feb	Mar	Apr	May
1	2	3	4	5	6	7	8	9	10	11	12			
	1	2	3	4	5	6	7	8	9	10	11	12		
		1	2	3	4	5	6	7	8	9	10	11	12	

• • •

Caution:

A rolling forecast is a viable forecasting technique to use when faced with quickly evolving markets or changes in your internal operations, but be careful that it doesn't become an excuse for sloppy forecasting. There's a danger that people may not take the forecast seriously since they know it will be frequently adjusted anyway. Moreover, if your "forecast" also serves as your sales budget, as is often the case, then continually shifting your sales targets may confuse or de-motivate your managers, sales people and other staff. You need to decide for yourself how much stability you need in your forecast, whether it's monthly, bi-monthly, quarterly, semi-annual or annual.

A final point is that reassessing your sales forecast at frequent intervals can consume significant time and resources internally, and thereby distract employees from their main operational tasks. Is it worth the extra time and money?

• • •

PART IV:

How to Forecast, Step-by-Step

I n my opinion, it usually helps to be aware of the steps when working towards a goal. Rather than approaching building your sales forecast in an unstructured way, therefore, I recommend that you follow a series of steps and that you are aware of each step as your perform it.

How to forecast step-by-step

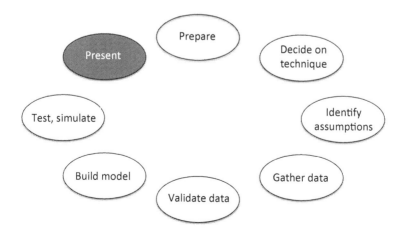

Step 1: Prepare

Before you begin, it helps to prepare. That means considering some of the issues I mentioned in *PART II: What to consider before you begin* such as defining your market, deciding whether it makes sense to extrapolate or not, and the important characteristics of your market (size, rate of growth, price development, etc.).

Step 2: Decide on Technique

Next, you can decide which of the 16 techniques I've presented would be most appropriate to your situation. Refer to *PART II: What to consider before you begin* for some helpful hints on what to consider when deciding which technique to use, as well as the information on the 16 techniques themselves.

Step 3: Identify Assumptions

This is one of the most important of all steps. Identify your assumptions as explicitly as possible. This is a crucial step as your assumptions underpin your entire model. The best thing to do is to write them down. As the saying goes in the IT world: "if it's not written down, it doesn't exist."

Step 4: Gather Data

You can gather data from any number of different sources: market reports, internal IT systems, internal reports or paper repositories, market research surveys, trade journals, online databases and your own investigations.

Step 5: Validate Data

Validate your data in much the same way you would validate your model. For example:

- Check the credibility of the data source
- Check the absolute and relative magnitudes of the data

• Check the accuracy of data against other datasets

Step 6: Build Model

Build your model, whether in a spreadsheet, software program or even by hand. If necessary, write some documentation so that the different components or your model are clearly identified as well as the different steps. For example, you might have different tabs or different sections on your spreadsheet dedicated to different calculations: calculating market size, forecasting your sales volume, etc. It often helps to have a separate area where you list all the variables that need to be specified or input as opposed to those that are calculated. Alternatively, you can highlight them visually in some way.

Step 7: Test and Simulate

Don't skip this step. It will help you to refine your model. Run some simulations with different data to see how your model works and whether it makes sense.

We deal with this in more detail in *PART V: How to validate your forecast*.

Step 8: Present your Forecast

Your last step would be to present your sales forecast, whether to an internal or external audience. We discuss this in more detail in *PART VI: Presenting your forecast*.

I've presented this process as a sequence, but it's not necessarily sequential. You may perform the steps in a different order; you may go back and repeat a step before you move on. This is just a rough guide. Don't assume that you have to follow these exact steps in the order shown here.

PART V:

How to validate your forecast

I can't emphasize enough how important it is to validate your forecast. Validating your forecast will not only improve its accuracy, it will also enhance your own understanding of the forecast model and your industry's dynamics. It's really worth spending some time on this, not just considering your job done once you have the forecast results.

Test scenarios

How do you validate a forecast? One thing you can do is to test scenarios. This is quite common with spreadsheet models. Try changing different variables. There's actually a scenario function in Excel that let's you define the changing cells so that you can easily change various variables.

> **Your scenarios should tell a story."**

It's also helpful to define discrete scenarios. Write them down. Don't just change numbers robotically, but actually write down the assumptions behind them and describe what's happening in the market that results in the change in that particular variable. For example, your "High-growth" scenario could assume that you introduce a new product with features that no competitor is able to match or that your new production process gives you a unique cost advantage. Your scenarios should tell a story.

The most common approach is to have an optimistic, a pessimistic and a base case, and I often follow this approach myself. However, you don't need to limit yourself to these three cases that stretch across the spectrum of possible outcomes. You could also have scenarios, whether they're optimistic or pessimistic, that are based on different market events such as changes in technology, consumer

You could also have scenarios, whether they're optimistic or pessimistic, that are based on different market events such as changes in technology, consumer preferences, competition or regulation."

preferences, competition or regulation. The market could evolve along any number of different paths. Try to define several different paths and then decide how they could be reflected by your variables in numerical terms (for example, intensified competition will cause our average price to fall by 10%).

Check magnitudes

Besides testing various scenarios, you may also check the absolute and relative magnitudes of results. If you get absolute magnitudes that seem wildly optimistic or inflated, for example, you may want to re-examine your assumptions or the logic of your model. The same goes for relative magnitudes. For example, imagine that sales of your new product are simply far too high relative to total market growth. That could be a red flag that either your assumptions are overly optimistic or that the logic of your model is flawed or both.

By the same token, sometimes you may get a result that seems extreme but is actually accurate. Your sales may be doubling every year, for example, but perhaps this is a reasonable assumption because of the introduction of a disruptive technology, change in consumer tastes or new regulations. Obviously, you need to decide for yourself what's reasonable.

Check against actual historical data

Actual experience is a litmus test. See what actually happened in the past and how that might apply in this future case. You can compare your results with actual historical data drawn from your other products, from your competition's products, or even from a completely different industry that is somehow comparable. For example, the opera house industry is somewhat similar to the airline industry. At first blush, this sounds like a ridiculous claim but if you stop to consider the business drivers of each industry, you'll see that they are both driven to a certain extent by the need to fill capacity. Capacity utilization is a key business driver whether you're offering Pavarotti performances or getting from point A to point B. Think how you could apply any relationships identified to your sales forecast logic.

Try to find industries that have a similar evolution. In hi-tech, for example, the evolution of the market for smartphones has probably been very similar to the evolution of the market for the telephone, except perhaps that the rate of diffusion for the smartphone is much higher; the market has reached maturity within a much shorter timeframe.

Use ratios as indicators

Another trick is to use ratios as indicators. Changes in these indicators or their relative magnitudes will give you clues as to the reasonableness of your forecast. For example, when you forecast your sales, also track you market share to see how it evolves. Does it suddenly double? Can you justify the doubling? What about annual sales? Are they growing at a rate that is ten times the growth rate of the overall market?

Summary of key concepts

Validate your sales forecast to improve its accuracy as well as your understanding of the forecast model and your industry's dynamics.

- **Test scenarios**: create discrete scenarios based on potential market events – don't limit yourself to "optimistic", "pessimistic" and "base case". Make sure that changes in variables reflect actual potential market events (e.g. a new product introduction boosts market share) rather than being just robotic manipulations of numbers. Your scenarios should tell a story.

- **Check magnitudes**: check both absolute and relative magnitudes; use your judgment and market knowledge to decide what's reasonable.

- **Check against actual historical data**: actual experience is a litmus test. Compare your sales performance with what happened in the past, either for your product or a comparable one.

- **Use ratios as indicators**: devise ratios and monitor changes in them to give you indications of the reasonableness of your forecast.

PART VI:

Presenting your forecast

P resenting your forecast is in some ways the most important thing you'll do. You may have invested a huge amount of time and energy in producing your forecast, but if you're not able to communicate it effectively and convincingly, then all your time and effort will have been for naught. With this in mind, it seems wise to spend some time thinking about how to best present your forecast.

Do your homework

If you've done your homework, it should be relatively easy to give a strong presentation. When I say "homework", I mean you've considered your market and chosen the forecasting technique that best fits with it; you've identified your assumptions explicitly; you've validated your data so you know that it is reasonable; and you've tested various scenarios.

Be conservative

You should also be conservative or cautious in forecasting. When they make forecasts, many entrepreneurs tend to be wildly over-optimistic. Perhaps this is why some venture capitalists, when they review a sales forecast from an entrepreneur, automatically slice it by half. They just know that entrepreneurs tend to be over-optimistic.

Analyze your audience

It pays to think about your audience. What are their agendas? What's driving them? Are they receptive to your proposal or are they skeptical? Who might oppose you and to what are they most likely to object?

Be transparent

Explain the thinking behind your model. Remember I said that a model should not be a black box? You should be able to explain the key drivers underpinning your model. Which are the key variables? Be able to explain your model to people so that they can understand it. Don't keep this information to yourself out of a fear that people will then critique your

People tend to become uncomfortable with the unknown; the known or familiar gives them a warm and fuzzy feeling."

model or out of complacency that no one but you can understand it. It's better to have a very clear and solid logic that you can explain to your audience so that they can understand your thought process. There's some psychology behind this: people tend to become uncomfortable with the unknown; the known or familiar gives them a warm and fuzzy feeling. I bet you never thought that your dry forecasting model could do that!

Present scenarios

If you've produced multiple scenarios as I've suggested, then present some or all of them. Scenarios tend to show the boundaries or extremes of your model and its different dimensions. You might also present a scenario that is a "straw man". A straw man is defined by dictionary.com as: "a fabricated or conveniently weak or innocuous person, object, matter, etc., used as a seeming adversary or argument." You would create a straw man scenario that is either one that is very unattractive to your audience or one that they think is not reasonable (be careful not to be too unreasonable, however, or you will lose credibility). Then you would present the scenario that you think is reasonable and that is the one that you want to promote. Your audience may more readily accept your preferred scenario because they'll contrast it with the one which they didn't like or believe.

Summary of key concepts

Thinking about how best to present your forecast will increase the chances of it being accepted. Then your hard work won't go to waste.

- **Do your homework**: if you've done things like chosen the forecasting technique that best suits your market and identified your assumptions explicitly, then it should be relatively easy to give a strong presentation.

- **Be conservative**: err on the side of caution; don't over-estimate your sales, rates of growth or other variables.

- **Analyze your audience**: know what their concerns are and how to overcome any potential objections.

- **Be transparent**: make it easy for people to understand your model and they'll feel more comfortable with it. End result: they'll be more likely to believe it.

- **Present scenarios**: a range of possible scenarios is more credible than a single view and gives your audience the chance to select the one that they find most credible. It also opens up the possibility of constructive dialogue.

PART VII:

"What if's?"

I n building a model and making a sales forecast, it's normal to run into obstacles. I call these "what if's?". Let's identify some of the most common "what if's?" and see how they can be addressed.

What if I lack reliable data?

If you lack reliable data but have the time, budget and inclination, just do some market research. Of course, when I say market research it could be anything from just calling up five customers (e.g. if the number of customers in your industry is very limited and you're only selling 15 systems a year) or it could be conducting a full-blown market survey. You could also perhaps buy a market survey off-the-shelf without having to commission one. You could use data from comparable products or services. You could extrapolate. You could guesstimate (make an intelligent guess to fill-in holes in your data).

What if people raise objections to my forecast?

There are two ways to deal with objections:

- **Pre-empt**: if you've done your homework and tested your model thoroughly, you can be pretty sure that it's solid. If you've created scenarios as I've suggested, then you could present your audience with several different scenarios. Then, even if they object to one scenario, they may support another. There will be something in one of the scenarios that they'll like or find to be believable. In a way, there will be a scenario for everyone. Hopefully, you can steer them towards a consensus. While some people will support one scenario more than another, the group's view will hopefully converge around a particular scenario (or adaptation of one). At least then your model has become a tool for discussion and exploration of the market dynamics rather than being rejected outright. You should also explain upfront very clearly how your model works, what the assumptions are, where you got the data, how reliable the data is, etc.

- **Respond**: when people raise objections, don't get defensive. Instead, respond to any valid critique of your model. By responding, you don't necessarily have to throw out your entire model. You may just need to adjust your variables or use different data. In the end, you may be able to address the concerns of your critics simply by tweaking some variables, changing the logic of your model slightly, or applying a different data set.

What if it's a completely new market?

As I've suggested before, you can get around this by drawing parallels with existing or historical markets. Many innovations, for example, follow a similar path of diffusion (often an S-curve). The markets for products as diverse as the combustion engine, the telephone and the smartphone have probably followed similar trajectories (albeit over vastly different time-frames).

You might also apply *Technique #10: Modeling* or *Technique #11: Growth Pattern-fitting*.

You could also explore multiple scenarios. See which scenario makes the most sense for this market. At least you would explore the boundaries of possible sales and the evolution of the market, instead of limiting yourself to a single view.

What if the market is evolving so fast that I can't forecast more than one or two periods ahead?

This can happen in very quickly evolving markets. Develop scenarios but also consider increasing the granularity of your forecast: forecasting at a more detailed level, such as for individual product categories or by month rather than by year. You could also use *Technique #16: Rolling Forecast* to increase the accuracy of your forecast despite the rapid changes in the market.

What if I'm forecasting for a non-standard product or service?

Consider defining standard bundles of the service or standard configurations or packages of the product. Some people may be reluctant to do this, especially for services, but it's actually not that unreasonable to do. If you really scrutinize your offer, most of the time you'll be able to see that you offer specific bundles of services over and over again. Once you've created standard bundles or packages, you can assign average prices to each bundle or package, and perhaps forecast each one separately.

Summary of key concepts

Here are some common obstacles and how to over-come them:

- **What if I lack reliable data?** Do market research, use data from comparable products or services, or extrapolate.

- **What if people raise objections to my forecast?** Preempt objections by clearly identifying your assumptions, validating your data and testing your model thoroughly. Respond to any valid critique by adjusting variables, changing assumptions, using a different dataset or adapting your logic.

- **What if it's a completely new market?** Draw parallels with other markets, whether existing or historical. Explore multiple scenarios. Use *Technique #10: Modeling* or *Technique #11: Growth Pattern-fitting*.

- **What if the market is evolving so fast that I can't forecast more than one or two periods ahead?** Develop scenarios, increase the granularity of your forecast or use *Technique #16: Rolling Forecast*.

- **What if I'm forecasting for a non-standard product or service?** Define standard bundles and assign each one an average price. Forecast each one separately, if necessary, for greater overall accuracy.

CONCLUSION

A recurring theme throughout this book has been that sales forecasting is more "art" than "science". While it helps to be aware of the various techniques, ultimately your sales forecast will only be as good as the assumptions that underpin it and the data that you feed into your model. It's up to you to interpret the market and decide how you think your business could perform within it. With this in mind, it bears repeating that it's essential to create discrete scenarios based on potential market developments (scenarios are market "stories"), to write down your assumptions, to validate your data, and to test your model. The information contained in this book should help you accomplish all of the above.

Some people seem to have a natural "feel" for the market. I'm not sure whether it's based on years of experience, natural intuition or both. Even such market "geniuses" risk calling the market incorrectly, however, if there is a disruptive change in the market. You don't need to be a market genius yourself, provided that you are able to recognize one when you meet him or her, and that you know when to follow his or her predictions, and when not to.

At the other end of the spectrum is the approach of a former boss of mine who always insisted: "Show me the data!" This approach also has its merits, especially since, in my experience, some managers make bold statements without a shred of evidence to support them. Sometimes these pronouncements are driven by politics. Be careful that your sales forecast does not become captive to someone's hidden agenda.

As a sales forecaster, you need to be what I would call a "pragmatic purist". "Pragmatic" in the sense of using any information or technique which you deem helpful; "purist" in the sense of trying to create the most accurate forecast possible while being as transparent as possible about the assumptions, logic, data and other elements behind it. My final advice to you would be: back up every conclusion with data that is as solid as possible, as my ex-boss would have demanded, but leave space for interpretation and for your intuition. As the pioneering technologist Alan Kay once said: "the best way to predict the future is to invent it."

The best way to predict the future is to invent it."

• • •

If you have any questions or comments, or for further information, please visit: www.salesforecasting.biz.

INDEX

A

Accounting rules, 2

Annual sales, 3

Assumptions, xi, 4, 5, 9, 13, 48, 51, 53, 55, 60, 63, 64

B

Book-to-bill ratio, 27

C

Competition, 3, 35, 38, 52, 53

Conversion rate, 28

D

Data collection, 18

Data collection system, 18

E

Exponential curve, 32

Extrapolate, 48, 59

F

Forecast window, 44

H

Historical data, 25, 33, 53

I

Inflection points, 32

Installed base, ix, 3, 39

L

Leading indicator, 27

Lifetime, 17, 34, 38

Load factor, 28

M

Market growth, 9

Market share, 3

Market size, 9

Market stage, 10

Moving average, 23

MS-Excel, 25

P

Penetration, 3, 36

Price development, 10

Price elasticity, 41, 42, 43, 44

Price sensitivity, 41, 42

R

Regulatory environment, 10

Replacement purchases, 38

Replacement rate, 17, 37, 39

Revenue passenger miles or kilometers, 28

Rolling forecast, 44

Run rate, 22

S

Sales budget, 46

Sales people, 16, 46

Sales per square foot, 28

Sales recognition, 2

Saturation, 36

Scenarios, 6, 51, 52, 55, 57, 60, 61, 63

S-curve, 32, 60

Seasonal, 2, 32

Seasonality, 9, 21

Straw man, 57

T

Technology, 10

Trend fitting, 25

Trendline, 25

U

Units, 1, 34

V

Validation, 18

Value, 1

Volume, 1

82183231R00044

Made in the USA
Middletown, DE
01 August 2018